How to be an Estate & Letting Agent

by

Rob Bryer

The Professional Agent Academy

Copyright © 2015 Rob Bryer

All rights reserved.

ISBN-13: 978-1515199427

ISBN-10: 1515199428

The information provided in this guide is intended to give you the basics in order to get started. The Professional Agent Academy has made every attempt to ensure the accuracy and reliability of the information provided. However, the information is provided "as is" without warranty of any kind.

How to be an Estate & Letting Agent

CONTENTS

1	Introduction	9
2	The TGEA Network	11
3	Systems, Software and Essential Equipment	13
4	Marketing – Getting Started	17
5	Setting Your Fees	18
6	General Policies & Procedures	21

Section II Lettings

7	Overview	25
8	What is the role of the Letting Agent?	26
9	Marketing the Property	32
10	The Tenant Application Process	33
11	The Move In	37
12	The Inventory	38
13	Summary of Lettings Procedure	41

Section III Estate Agency

14	Overview	43
15	Weekly Marketing Plan	51
16	Market Appraisals and Valuations	53
17	Marketing Your properties	59
18	The Offer and Acceptance	65
19	Summary of Sales Procedure	74
20	Conclusion and further study	75

Forward

Congratulations on choosing this guide provided by The Professional Agent Academy.

The journey you are about to embark upon offers you one of the most exciting and lucrative industries you can enter today.

This guide provides you with the skills and inspiration to get started in this business. As you progress further learning is available from The Professional Agent Academy to enhance your skills.

This guide is designed to provide you with the knowledge to get started as an estate and letting agent.

Whether you are looking to set up on your own or within the TGEA network (our done for you option via The Good Estate Agent) we have all the information you need to succeed.

We look forward to seeing you work your way up the ladder to a very profitable career.

Good Luck!

Rob Bryer
The Professional Agent Academy

www.professionalagentacademy.co.uk

Section I
General

Introduction

The aim of this guide is to get you up and running as quickly as possible by providing you with the skills and knowledge you need to succeed.

If you join our membership program you will also be provided with support from your mentor during your training and development as an Agent.

First we look at the systems and software you will be using and the equipment you need before reviewing essential policies and procedures.

Next we will look at the various ways to market yourself and the business. It is vital you start thinking about your marketing plan from day one to ensure your success.

It's entirely up to you but we recommend you study both our sales and lettings guides. Even if you do not wish to conduct business in both areas you may still need some basic knowledge later on in your career. There are many cross sale opportunities available such as landlords wishing to sell their properties.

Once these sections have been completed you are ready to go but we also recommend all agents to become National Federation of Property Professional qualified.
We provide courses on these advanced subjects as and when you require them.

THE TGEA Network

We realise that not everyone wants the hassle and cost of setting up their own agency from scratch.

This is why we created the TGEA Network, a done for you solution providing a platform for agents to work from without the hassle and cost of setting up their own agency.

TGEA members run their own business but the network supplies and pays for the following:

Advertising on Rightmove and Zoopla
Admin support including:

>Telephone answering
>Enquiry management
>Admin Support
>Tenancy creation
>Property Management

In fact TGEA members only have to worry about taking properties on and conducting viewings. Everything else is covered.

Agents pay a percentage of income for this service and can also grow their own team within the network. If you are not already a member get in touch to find out more.

Throughout this guide you will see the information in a box when the information applies to TGEA Network members.

> **TGEA NETWORK:**
>
> Information in this box applies to TGEA network members only.

Find out about joining at ProfessionalPropertyAcademy.co.uk

Systems, Software and Essential Equipment

Telephone System

The telephone is one of your most important tools in this business.

Whether you use a mobile phone or a landline you want to create a professional impression to your customers.

Using Voip technology you can easily get low cost and professional telephone system set up. Whether you just want one line or multiple lines we recommend using a service such as voipfone.co.uk

This system and systems like it allow you to set up new phone lines from just a couple of pounds per month. You can use a software phone and headphones with your PC or purchase a hardwired phone such as the Snom 300.

Voicemail can be routed to an email and calls can be forwarded to a telephone answering service while you are out.

Make sure all voicemail greetings including those on your mobile are professional.

You never want to miss a call.

> **TGEA NETWORK:**
>
> Members of the TGEA network have all their calls answered by our head office team.
>
> We use a sophisticated telephone system which allows you to connect to our telephone network from anywhere in the world.
>
> This allows for advanced functions such as call transfer, queuing, automatic call routing etc.

Emails

You should make sure you have a professional email address. A Hotmail or Gmail address can look unprofessional.

When you setup your website you should also create a company email address for example yourname@yourcompany.com

We recommend using a Google Domain for our your email system. This allows you to access emails from anywhere and from any device and create multiple email addresses for your company.

Visit https://www.google.com/work/apps/business/ for more information.

There are also a number of useful tools available such as Google apps which will allow you to share documents, spread-sheets etc.

You should avoid using your email for personal use as this can cause your inbox to become cluttered. This can also increase cases of spam and potential security risks.

To maintain professionalism company business should always be transacted via your company email address and not a personal account.

> **TGEA NETWORK:**
>
> TGEA members will have an email address setup for them as this is all handled by the network IT support team.

Property Management System

A good property management system will provide access to store all your client details (Landlords and Tenants), record details of viewings, record property information, upload your property pictures and publish pictures and text on to your website and publish these to various property portals.

There are various off the shelf products available such as Expert Agent, Gnomen and Aquaint.

> **TGEA NETWORK:**
>
> Members have access to our property management system.

Required Equipment

Digital Camera
Laser Measuring Device not sonic.
PC/laptop with broadband connection
All in one Printer/Scanner/Fax Machine
Mobile Phone

4. Marketing – Getting Started

Market Research

The methods, levels of service and fees charged by agents in different areas can vary dramatically.

Many agents provide a complex fee structure. This often means they will offer the landlord a very attractive base fee but when you look closer there are many add-ons for example for contracts, inventories etc.

Understanding this fully and being able to explain to your client will be crucial in helping you to win business against the competition so your first task is to Mystery Shop your competitors.

Being a new agent, you will have a huge advantage because you will be unknown and can gain a lot of information.

Exercise:

Using the following questions to conduct your own mystery shopping survey.

Questions:

What do you charge for letting only and what's included? Check for hidden extras.

What do you charge for full management and what's included?

How much do you charge tenants and what checks do you carry out?

There is a legal requirement for all agents to display fees on their websites however you will still find agents who do not do this. Picking up the phone is the best option as you will get a feel for how they are presenting their fees.

Setting Your Fees

Once you have your market research in hand you will be in a good position to set your own fees.

Don't just go in at the lowest price. You are an expert and need to be paid what you are worth.

You need to look at two sets of fees. Landlord Fees and Tenant Fees. The rules on tenants Fees vary throughout the UK. In England there are no restrictions but like landlord fees they must be displayed on your website and within your advertising.

Tenant Fees:

Tenant Application Fee (Per Tenant)

Guarantor Fee (If Required)

Check Out Fee (Sometimes paid on move in)

Tenancy Renewals   (paid by landlord, tenant or both)

Tenancy Agreement Preparation

Landlord Fees:

Initial letting fee – Typically 50-100% of the first months rent or a fixed fee

Monthly management fee (if managed) 10-15% of the rent.

Inventory Creation £75 - £150

Deposit Protection £30 - £50

AST Renewals (paid by landlord, tenant or both)

Other fees may be charged for example additional property visits, percentage of works on large refurbishment projects. Your market research will reveal the types of fees being charged.

General Policies & Procedures

Below are the Policies and Procedures adopted by the TGEA Network. We have provided these policies and procedures as an example for your use.

General

All employees must comply with Policy & Procedures. Failure to comply may result in holding of commissions due and, if matters are not corrected dismissal.

I. Dress Code.

    a. All employees and associates are required to dress in an appropriate manner for their business role.
    b. Where a uniform is provided this must be worn on all company business.
    c. Shirts must be ironed and shoes polished to ensure a smart and professional appearance.

II. Keys

    a. All keys must be logged on the secure Key List
    b. Keys must be labelled with a code and must never show the property address.
    c. Key code should match the property ID on the Property Management System.
    d. Keys are valuable and to lose one is serious for the customer. Keys must always be kept in a secure place and efforts must be made to avoid the loss of a key. However, if a key is lost despite such efforts then it must be

reported immediately to your manager. Lost keys must be replaced and paid for by the person responsible for their loss.

III. Security

a. We take the security of our employees and contractors very seriously.
b. All appointments must be logged in the diary so we know where you are.
c. If you feel uncomfortable with doing an appointment just don't do it or make arrangements with a colleague to accompany you if necessary.
d. If you find yourself at an appointment and you feel unsafe please call the Head Office and advise that you are "Create Safety Phrase" after the appointment.
e. The security key phrase and will alert us of potential danger. We will send someone to the property to meet you.
f. Should you be the receiver of such a call please alert management immediately. Never place yourself in direct danger.

IV. The Property Ombudsman (TPO)

a. The company is a member of The Property Ombudsman.
b. All Staff & Associates are required to familiarise themselves with the code of practice and adhere to these guidelines at all times.

V. Complaints Procedure

a. All complaints either oral or in writing must be recorded on the client's file.
b. Your immediate line manager must be informed.
c. The customer must be given a copy of the complaints procedure.
d. All written complaints must be acknowledged in writing within 3 working days as per TPO guidelines.
e. A formal written outcome must be sent to the Complainant within 15 working days. A senior member of staff not directly involved with the transaction should deal with the complaint.
f. If the Complainant remains dissatisfied, he must be told how he can further pursue his complaint within your business. This should provide the opportunity for a speedy, separate and detached review of the complaint by staff not directly involved in the transaction. Such a review must be sent to the Complainant within 15 working days.
g. Following the conclusion of your investigation, a written statement of your final view, and

including any offer made, must be sent to the Complainant. This letter must also tell the Complainant how the matter can be referred to the Ombudsman, pointing out that any such referral by the Complainant must be made within 6 months of your final view.

h. You must not imply that payment of any outstanding commission fee or additional costs is a pre-condition of a review by the Ombudsman.

SECTION II
Lettings

Overview

This is an overview of the Lettings Industry will provide you with the necessary knowledge to begin trading as a Letting Agent.

> **TGEA NETWORK:**
>
> Whilst many of the items will be dealt with by our administration staff it is important that you have a working knowledge of the processes involved. Items marked with a * will be dealt with by the admin staff. All referencing, contract creation and inventories will be handled by the administration team unless your assistance is required i.e. to collect identification.

As a Letting Agent your primary role will be to:

- Prospect for Landlords/Properties
- Sign Up Landlords
- Take details and photographs of properties
- Health & Safety, Fire & Furnishings Check
- Upload details to the Property Management System
- Book viewings*
- Conduct Viewings
- Reference Tenants*
- Draw up tenancy agreements*
- Collect Rent & Deposits*

- Check in new Tenants
- Conduct Periodic Checks
- Check out Tenants
- Deal with issues during the tenancy*

What is the role of the Letting Agent?

As a letting agent your primary responsibility is to your client i.e. 'The Landlord'.

The Landlord's property is a valuable asset and they are trusting you to find a suitable tenant who will look after that asset and treat it with respect.

You need to be aware of the Landlord's legal responsibilities so that you can advise and make sure they adhere to them.

Landlord's Responsibilities:

Gas Safety – Certification by recognized authority required.
Fire & Furnishings Certificates Required for all Soft Furnishings including Mattresses
Non- Resident Landlords' Tax Implications
Mortgage Consent
Energy Performance Certificates (EPC's)
Buildings Insurance
Council Tax
Income Tax
Electrical Certificates (Not always required but advisable)
Fire Alarm Certificates (Not always required but advisable)

You will offer two main letting services.

Letting Only

You find tenants, reference them, prepare contracts and an inventory and collect the initial rent and deposit. You check in the tenants and advise utility suppliers of the change of occupier/s. The rest is left to the Landlord.

Fully Managed Letting

As above but you take care of rental collection, periodic checks and any issues relating to the property. Each Landlord's requirements differ but typically you will be given authority to carry out repairs up to £100 without prior authorisation.

Marketing and Mystery Shopping

It is important that you remember to carry out the marketing and mystery shopping guidance (refer to page 16) so you have a good idea of your market place.

Taking on your first property

Normally the first step to renting a property is an appointment to give a rental valuation.

Frequently Landlords will know or will have a good idea what they want to achieve for their property however it is best practice to provide market comparables.

You can do this easily by researching the internet for similar properties in the area.

The following websites will be useful in your search:

Zoopla.co.uk
Findaproperty.co.uk
Rightmove.co.uk

Do not be afraid to challenge your Landlord's valuation as they may not always be right and it is pointless for both you and the Landlord to try and market a property over its value.

Make sure the rental figure is going to meet your Landlord's needs and that it does not expose them to financial risk i.e. shortfall on mortgage and additional costs of maintaining a property. Sometimes this is not possible but it is best practice to ensure your Landlord is aware of the risks.

Complete a property fact find with the Landlord and take photographs.

Give the landlord an "Advice for Landlords" document as this contains important information about their legal responsibilities. (see examples at professionalpropertyacademy.co.uk)

Referring to the previous listed requirements as we must ensure that we check out the following:

Gas Certificate

You must have a copy of the Gas Certificate from a Gas Safe engineer. One copy must also remain at the property.

You can arrange this for the Landlord if at all possible.

Electrical Certificate

Whilst this is not a legal requirement it is best practice to have one. You should advise all Landlords to organise the necessary checks and therefore safeguard both themselves and their tenants against any potential problems. It is not hugely expensive (typically £150) and it could save a life. For some properties such as HMO's (Houses in Multiple Occupation) this is a legal requirement. Any properties supplied with electrical goods need to have an annual PAT test.

Insurance

You must advise Landlords to ensure they have appropriate Landlords' buildings and insurance and you should obtain a copy for your records. It is also advisable to have a small amount of Landlords' contents cover.

Mortgage Consent

You should see sight of 'consent to let' from the mortgage company if the property is mortgaged. This will also detail any interested parties on the property.

Deposits

All deposits must be held in a government authorised scheme. There are a number of these but we recommend

using the Deposit Protection Service.
This service is free however you can charge an administration fee for processing a deposit. The landlord may take care of the deposit themselves but this must be held in an approved scheme or they may be liable for a fine of up to 3 x the deposit amount. You are responsible for ensuring that if they do this themselves that you have written a letter to the Landlord confirming that they understand their obligations in this regard.

Within 30 days of receiving a deposit you must give information to the tenant regarding which scheme is being used. There is a specific document known as the prescribed information that must be signed by the tenant.

At the end of the tenancy both parties must agree that there are no deductions to be made, due to damage for example, before the DPS releases the deposit. In the event of a dispute this can be resolved by a voluntary dispute service or by the courts. But of course your job will be to try to avoid this by an amicable arrangement – remembering that your duty is to the Landlord.

House in Multiple Occupation - HMO's

The rules on HMO's can vary depending on your local council. You should contact your local council to get clarification. They should be able to provide a Landlords handbook.

A house in multiple occupation is a building, occupied by three or more people, living as more than one household.

A household is a group of people who live together. They

must be connected by marriage, be related – a child, parent, sister, brother, nephew, niece or in-law for instance – or have another recognised connection such as fostering or adoption.

People that live in this place, but are not connected in this way, are not counted as a single household. So, for example, a group of five students or adult friends count as five households, even if they live at the same address and share facilities.

Many HMO's require licensing. If unsure contact your local housing department rather than hoping for the best.

There are many requirements for HMO's including minimum room sizes, fire safety regulation and door lock requirements. For more information refer to the HMO handbook.

Marketing the Property

The Landlord will expect the Letting Agent to fully market their property for letting.

The Letting Agent should consider the following methods to achieve a let.

- 'To Let' Boards
- Property to Let Listing
- Web portals

Your first step into advertising should be featuring your rental property on the your website and the property portals..

Landlords - helpful hints

With experience, a letting agent will know when it is appropriate to terminate a Landlord's agreement. Some Landlords may have unrealistic expectations and it will be in everyone's interests to part company. Remember to make sure that you are as clear as possible when outlining your responsibilities and offering your services.

Ensure that the property is in a let-able condition. Ensure that any pending jobs are completed by the Landlord before showing the property to prospective tenants, sometimes Landlords will forget to complete these jobs and you may inherit a property with issues.

Where possible, ensure that everything works, i.e. all taps flow water, the toilet flushes, doors are lockable, windows can open, the heating system heats the property, the hot water system provides hot water, electricity is available at the property etc., as this prevents telephone complaints when the tenant moves in. Try to do everything you can to avoid this happening.

Remember the property will usually 'sell its self. If the property is in poor condition, you may have problems in letting which will result in many telephone calls from an irate and disappointed landlord asking why their property has not let. Ensure that the property is 'up to scratch' when you take it on.

The Tenant Application Process

Basic Tenant requirements should be established

- Location/Area
- Number of bedrooms
- Garden
- Parking
- Amenities
- Rent - budget per month

In addition to the usual residential needs for Letting we also may need to establish the client's situation re these issues

- Smoking/Non Smoking
- Children
- Pets

The skill of understanding both tenants' and Landlords' requirements will help build good relationships. The ideal situation being for both parties to be more than satisfied with the outcome of the arrangement.
Needs should be matched with suitable rental properties and the property management system is a tool that can help you achieve this.

Once a prospective tenant has viewed a property and decided that they wish to proceed, you must then follow the process outlined below.

If you have several persons interested in the property at the same time then you should advise them that the first person to reserve the property with a Tenant Administration fee will be referenced and have priority over the property.

It is not 'good practice' to put several tenants through the referencing process for the same property at the same time. Disappointment could lead to complaints.

Your prospective tenant is responsible for paying the costs of their reference check and this is called the Tenant Application fee.

Before you reference your prospective tenant, there are a couple of checks that you should carry out to ensure as far as you are able, that the tenant is actually in a position to secure a tenancy.

- Your tenants must have had 6 months continuous employment at time of application unless they are deemed to be in a professional position such as Doctor or Lawyer.

- Your tenants must have an annual income that is 2.5 times that of the rent of the property they want. So for example if the monthly rent is £500 the tenant must be earning £500 x 12 months x 2.5 = £15,000. If the tenant does not meet this income level and is part of a couple you can do a joint application, however both parties must pay the referencing cost.

- Students and unemployed persons will automatically require a guarantor. The income needed for a guarantor is 3 times the rent required.

- An unemployed tenant who is receiving housing benefit should provide a copy of their 'pre-determination' form from the local authority. If the unemployed person is of independent means they will be asked to provide evidence of savings equal to that of the total rental period of the agreement x 3. i.e. 6 months tenancy agreement of £1000 per month = £6,000 x 3 = £18,000

- They must provide a 'proof of residency' at their current address. The only proofs of residency you should accept are:
    - A driving license showing the current address;
    - A recent (no older than 3 months) gas, electric, water, telephone/mobile phone bill;
    - A recent Council Tax bill showing the applicant's name and current address;

o A letter on headed paper from the personnel / human resources department of the employer confirming current address - this letter must be signed and dated by the payroll department or the financial director and contain the printed name and position of the signatory.'

If your prospective tenant meets the above criteria then you may proceed to put them through the referencing process.

There are various companies that provide referencing services and can take care of the whole process for you. Most will also offer rent and legal guarantee's that you can sell to the landlord.

> **TGEA NETWORK:**
>
> Our tenant application form is on our website and the whole process is taken care of by our admin team.

Most reference applications are processed within 2-3 working days, so ensure you manage your tenants' expectations on the turn-around process. Stress the importance of ensuring that their employer is ready to respond quickly to an employment reference request as this is where many reference applications slow down.

It should be noted that if a tenant has paid a holding deposit for a property but fails the reference check they are generally not entitled to a refund. You should make them aware that the fee is non-refundable under this circumstance. If the Landlord pulls out of letting the property, the tenant would expect to receive their holding deposit back in full, including any referencing costs. These costs should then be met by the Landlord. Once the tenant has passed the reference then you are ready to move them in!

The Move In

It is imperative that all your documentation is correctly completed and securely filed. Prior to handing over keys to your tenant, you must ensure that you have the following fully completed documents:

- Completed inventory
- Rental Agreement
- Information for tenants in the event of emergencies and contacts

We must have obtained a security deposit and first month's rent prior to handing over keys to your tenant. Do not provide keys to any tenant who has not paid in full.

Please ensure that you get 2 copies of all the documentation signed, the Tenant must sign both sets, retaining one copy whilst you should retain a copy in your file.

Ensure that all your documentation is secure - do not lose any documentation! Any Rent & Legal expenses claims will require completed copies of all paperwork as evidence.

On the rental agreement itself all named persons must sign in full on the last page otherwise paperwork will be void.

If there is a guarantor for the agreement they must sign in

the designated area.

Please note the documents may be signed in advance of the date of entry if this is easier for them, however this does not entitle them to gain possession of the property prior to the date which is on the lease agreement.

The Inventory

Prior to letting, a complete inventory and schedule of condition of the property should be prepared. This can be done either by the landlord, the agent or an inventory clerk

The Professional Agent Academy provides a further course on completing a thorough inventory. Find out more at professionalagentacademy.co.uk

The Inventory and Statement of Condition, is the most important weapon in the letting agent's armoury if things start to go wrong. Because it protects the Landlord, tenant and agent alike, one cannot over-stress the necessity for the utmost diligence in its preparation. Unfortunately, this vital document does not always receive the attention it deserves. The end result is invariably a dispute which can become acrimonious, with both sides blaming the agent for actual, or supposed, deficiencies. At the very least, the Landlord or agent may spend an inordinate amount of time endeavoring to resolve the dispute. At worst, the dispute may only be resolved by court or arbitration proceedings.

Purpose

The Inventory forms an agreement between the Landlord and tenant as to the true condition and contents of the property at the date of entry by the tenant. It will be used, when the tenancy terminates, to determine any damage or obvious misuse of the property or contents.

Detail

The Inventory should be as detailed as possible and will record the condition of each room and every item in the room. The Inventory is a written description and not merely a list of contents. It has to paint a picture to reveal to someone who was not present, the true nature of the property's contents and condition.

How much detail is required will depend on the type of property and value of the contents. An expensive house, full of antiques, will clearly require much greater detail and clarity compared with a terraced house with nondescript furnishings. However, every property is a castle in the eye of the owner and a valuable asset so the more descriptive detail the better. The guiding principle is to be as precise as possible; 'Rosewood Chippendale cabinet with three drawers and gilt-edged top' is a better description than 'cabinet made of red wood'.

Post Move In

All documentation should be stored safely and ideally scanned and saved onto a password protected and backed up computer.

The monthly rental should be collected by standing order. The tenant should set this up immediately. Many tenants confuse standing order with Direct Debit and expect you to debit their account. Instructions for the tenant should be detailed in their welcome letter which should accompany the contract.

Write to the local authority confirming the change in name for Council Tax Bills and contact the relevant utility companies to advise of final readings for the Landlord's bill and to set up a new account for the tenant.

> **TGEA NETWORK:**
>
> This task is handled by the administration team.

Set up a reminder for the 3 month stage to carry out a property inspection.

Set up a reminder for two months prior to the end of the tenancy agreement to establish with your Landlord and tenant if the lease is going to be carried on or ended.

Establish with the landlord how much contact they would like. Some like regular updates whilst others prefer you just to get on with it. You will find it is very important to get this right.

Summary of Lettings Procedure

1. Sign up a landlord
2. Obtain ID and proof of residence
3. Create details and photograph
4. Check/Order EPC & Gas Certificate
5. Publish property
6. Book viewings
7. Carry out viewings
8. Tenants complete referencing online.
9. Tenants pay Rent & Deposit
10. Inventory Booked
11. Move in day booked
12. Sign tenancy agreement and inventory, hand over keys and take meter readings (should be on inventory). Leave tenant with their copy.
13. Forward copies of documents to the Landlord.
14. Deduct fees and pay Landlord.
15. Utility Suppliers and Council advised.

16. Diarise periodic check for 3 months.

Example documentation can be found at professionalagentacademy.co.uk

This is just the beginning of your training. The next thing to do is to get out there and get some properties on. You will learn best on the job and Academy members will have the back up of my team and other agents to guide you through the process.

We also have further training modules available that will improve your knowledge and lead to industry recognised qualifications in both sales and lettings.

Good luck!

SECTION III

Estate Agency

Overview

AIM: To understand how to become a professional and successful Property Agent

Objectives

i) Understand the competition and learn some tools and tricks to help you with market research

ii) Know how get new business and undertake a market appraisal

iii) Be equipped to present your property portfolio to best advantage and know how to sell!

iv) Have an understanding of the art and importance of negotiation on behalf of your client and how to close deals

v) Steer your sales through to successful completion by understanding the importance of effective communication

vi) Know the importance of keeping records and know how to do it

vii) Master the rudiments of property legislation

UNDERSTAND THE COMPETITION AND LEARN SOME TOOLS AND TRICKS TO HELP YOU WITH MARKET RESEARCH

Everyone needs to know what they are up against when they start so the first crucial thing to do is to **understand your competition.** The second crucial thing to remember is that whatever you do, wherever you go, whoever you meet can present you with an **opportunity for doing business.**

You need to know you are offering services that are equal to, and with the aim of becoming better than, other estate agents in the area. There are several ways of doing this but you need to be systematic, keep records, share these with your managers, understand how to analyse your statistics and then act upon your findings.

DESK RESEARCH is one of the best ways to get a sense of what is on offer and it can be done without face to face, or telephone interaction. You can take your time and give yourself a chance to become familiar with prices and types of property in particular areas, to see which agent has the highest web profile, and email for information that can help you enormously to understand the services that agents offer.

MYSTERY SHOPPING is the next stage when you pick up the phone or go to a high street office to ask for some details as if you are a client wishing to sell or buy a property. You can ask about their fees, what sort of advertising material they use and where e.g. hard copy brochures, websites, which portals they use e.g. Rightmove, Prime Location etc. Do they do the viewings for you? What is their unique selling point?

Find out as much as you can about their **STANDARDS OF SERVICE** – what will they undertake to do for you and what professional bodies do they belong to.

When looking at the **MARKETING MATERIAL** note the quality of photography, whether or not they include floor plans, how good the descriptions are – spelling errors or professionally presented.

Ask them about their **MARKET SHARE** – where do they see themselves in relation to their own competition – 50% of the local houses for sale? 20%?

If you have a home of your own consider asking for a **MARKET APPRAISAL OR VALUATION** – you can then take note of their professionalism – promptness of arrival, attitude, personal appearance, questioning, how they take notes and conclude the visit, what happens next.

VISIT HIGH STREET BRANCHES in your local area and take note of how busy they are, how many properties are being advertised, any niche markets e.g. rural or equestrian properties, commercial etc. How welcoming are the staff, how do they take your particulars, how knowledgeable and helpful are they? Request **PROPERTY DETAILS** so that you can take it home and study it at your leisure.

What are their **OPENING HOURS** and how well-staffed are they and with **what LEVEL OF EXPERIENCE**

Are they open or closed during periods like **BANK HOLIDAYS**?

Making sense of your statistics

Take note of your competitors' total number of properties on the market and note them road by road, area by area. You should take a day out once a month just to do this and at the same time make the most of it by posting cards to advertise your own services.

What are the likely sources of agents' listed properties – do they advertise in local papers, number of boards, in shops, radio, word of mouth etc. You need to determine the reasons for success and emulate them. What are the reasons for people falling back – these are things to avoid!

KNOW HOW TO GET NEW BUSINESS AND UNDERTAKE A MARKET APPRAISAL

How to get new business from landlords and vendors by marketing yourself

By far the quickest and easiest way to get started in this business is to pick up the phone to existing landlords and occasionally vendors. But how do we find them?

Many landlords and some vendors will advertise their property privately as well as with local agents.

You can find private listings in your local newspapers and on websites such as Gumtree.co.uk

Use the landlord calling script available on the members website and you will be up and running in no time at all.

Other methods of attracting landlords/vendor

Networking

There are many networking groups out there and we would encourage you to join in. Most of these groups will allow you to visit once or twice before committing as a member.

BNI - http://www.bni-europe.com

BNI will only allow one trade type per group. This means if your trade is not taken you will get exclusivity. It is also a useful place to meet other trades useful to the business.

4Networking - http://www.4networking.biz/

4Networking has a slightly more flexible style and does not restrict to one trade per group only.

Who do you know?

Write a list of all the people you know and then pick up the phone to let them know what you are doing. Maybe they know someone wanting to let or sell their property. Your friends and family will want to support you. Perhaps they will be suitable candidates to expand your team.

Board Spotting & Board Knocking

Get out board spotting and take note of any To Let or For Sale boards. Drop a leaflet, letter or card through the door and keep following up weekly. If it's a sales property then knock on the door and introduce yourself.

There are a number of ways to board knock. Either be direct and offer your services and a free valuation or go for the softer approach by asking if you can help with their property search. Once you have contact details you can approach them about a valuation latter.

Leaflet Drops

Get out dropping leaflets through doors, putting them up in newsagents' windows and on notice boards.

Local Newsletters

Your local newsletter or school newsletters will welcome your advert and are normally very cost effective.

Referrals Once you get your business going make sure you ask for the referral. If you have done a good job for someone they will normally be more than happy to refer you.

Tenants

A tenant may be leaving another property they are letting so who is their landlord? Ask them and see if they can put you in touch.

Buyers

Remember many buyers are also sellers so keep in contact with them and encourage them to use your service. If you keep in touch with a buyer they are much more likely to remember you when it comes to switching agents.

Other Estate Agents & Letting Agents

Good estate and letting agents may be willing to sub out properties to you. Normally they would be prepared to pay you 20% of the first month's rent for finding them a suitable tenant. For sales they may offer up to 50% for a successful introduction. Independent agents are much more likely to co-operate in this way.

You may have Estate Agents in your area who have no interest in lettings and they may be willing to pass business to you on a split fee basis.

Trade Stands/Boot Fairs etc.

A good way to get out there and meet people is to book a stand. This could be from a school fair to a DIY store stand.

Costs will vary and ensure you have a range of promotional material to make your day a success.

Internet Advertising

Google, Facebook and twitter or all very viable methods of getting business. The best thing about these methods is that you only pay for results.

We run a number of online webinars on these subjects from basic setup to more advanced techniques.

The quickest and most effective marketing is to get on the phone, knock on doors and get out talking to people. Be persistent, follow up until they buy, die or go away!

Weekly Marketing Plan

Marketing is the single most important aspect of your business. Get out on the streets, get on the telephone, get out and meet people. This is a guide and you may need to change the days to suit i.e. when the local papers come out, when the local networking meetings are held.

Monday

Board Walk – Get out in your car or preferably your bike or on foot, and get down the names and addresses of all your competitors' boards. Post a letter through each door as you go and when you feel confident knock on the door and get chatting.

Tuesday

Grab the papers and pick up the phone.

This is really a lettings exercise as it's rare to find a private sale listing in the paper. This is a tried and tested method.

Also try websites such as Gumtree to find private listings.

See calling scripts on the members website.

Wednesday

General Canvassing. Get out with a batch of letters and hit the properties you know will sell. If you have a particular buyer in mind then this is all the better.

See letter templates at professionalpropertyacademy.co.uk

Thursday

The Existing Customer and Referrals.

Existing customers are gold. What more can we do for them and can they think of anyone who they could recommend us?

Of course you need customers first so look at the papers again for a second round, research property websites such as Gumtree and make some calls.

Friday

Friday is networking day. Networking really does work. There are many local options out there but my two favourites are the BNI and Rotary.

You can visit the BNI a couple of times free (although you may have to pay for your breakfast. Yes - this is an early start!) and I suggest you check out a number of groups before committing to one in particular.

Rotary International is more about charity and helping others in developing countries than about business. However, if you embrace it not only will it make you feel good but the people you meet will support you in everything you do. Many members are seasoned businessmen and women. I actually get a lot of business due to my association with Rotary members but I make sure I give back by helping the charitable aims.

Weekends are optional but I believe in quality time. You are not here to work yourself to death! You should be working to live not living to work!

Now plan your week and stick to it. Look at a 12 week plan and keep working on it.

Market Appraisals and Valuations

So – you have marketed yourself well and now have your first appointment to visit a house for a market appraisal and valuation. The approach for a sale or a rental property has many similarities and some major differences that will be outlined in the Sales and Lettings sections.

Here are the stages that you need to go through for either a sales or a lettings appointment.

1) **Whoever takes your booking should make sure they get full details about the property and the client.** You can do this on the form on the property management system and will include no of bedrooms, whether or not there is a garden, detached or semi, bungalow etc. The more information gained at this stage will mean you have a fuller picture to allow you to do some comparative valuations on-line or by historical research within your own team. If they have sold or let a house recently in the vicinity of your property then this will help you to make a judgement on the value. Knowing the motivation of the vendor or landlord

will also help – if it is a sale then maybe you can assist in property search too.

2) **Do some thorough research on comparable property.** If it is a sale property, print off some facts to demonstrate to your landlord or vendor recent prices so they have facts when the time comes to setting the price of their own property.

3) **If practical do a 'drive by'.** If you can drive past the property before doing a market appraisal you will not only be sure of finding it and making your appointment on time – you will have some valuable information about the state of the property from the outside. You can also familiarise yourself with the immediate surroundings – all important information to help you confidently approach your potential client.

4) **Telephone before you leave to confirm the appointment.** You will need to show that you are familiar with the area – schools, local facilities, transport links, etc., so that you can demonstrate your knowledge which will encourage the vendor or landlord that you can market the property effectively. Before leaving, make sure you have your marketing appraisal form, a contract and that you are smartly presented. You will need your measuring equipment and camera.

5) **Arrive promptly at the property.** Note the outside, any interesting features, front garden, drive etc. Introduce yourself and give your card. Suggest that

you go through the notes on the house that you have so far and complete the facts on your property appraisal and details form. This will help you build a rapport before being shown around. Without going overboard, note some positive things about the house that you can remark upon. Present any negative aspects of the property in a positive light where possible so that you can demonstrate your professionalism. After having been shown around go through the details of the sales or lettings contract. At this stage you need also to establish as far as you can the fixtures and fittings that are to be included in the price and any extra items that they would sell.

Confusion over what is going to be left behind can lead to disappointment and acrimony and could actually lose the deal. Despite the value of the property, relative to the value of lamp-shades, curtains etc., these items can overshadow the bigger picture – so do try to establish everything that is included early on and make sure items are listed in the brochure so that there is no room for argument later. You should point these items out when you produce the marketing brochure before advertising as a double check.

After you have looked around the house and noted all the details you now have your final marketing opportunity where you stress the unique factors about you and your company.

Tell the client how you will go about selling the property and discuss with them a marketing plan that is personalised to their house. Demonstrate which features should be highlighted and explain why they would be appealing. Suggest taking photographs and measurements today as this will mean the property can be marketed almost immediately. This is worth doing even if they haven't made a decision yet as it may help you win the deal. If they have had three agents around and don't have a particular favourite then it makes sense to go with the agent that doesn't need a second appointment to begin marketing.

You could make a follow-up appointment for photographs however if you think it would be a good idea to 'dress' or 'stage' the property. See the section on photographs below. Remember to ask them to allow a board by explaining that boards sell/let houses!

6) **Settle on a price and close the deal.** You will now need to discuss prices. Always ask the vendor or landlord if they have a price in mind. You can then explain to them why it is a good price or why it might be too high or too low. At this point you need to demonstrate your professionalism and be able to give good reasons for the price suggested. It

will be a waste of everyone's time if a house is over-priced as it will not sell, will linger on the market and ultimately the price will need to be reappraised and dropped which is disappointing for all concerned and time-wasting. Make sure you do not offend a potential client if you believe that the price they want is unrealistic. It is important to help your client understand the current market values. If they have any questions and you are unsure, rather than risk telling them something that may be incorrect, then tell them you will need to check and get back to them. Make sure you do! Ask them directly if they will allow you to have the property to sell or let and close the deal. Before signing an agreement to act on a client's behalf for the sale or the letting of property, you will need to agree commission. Make sure you know what the parameters are for negotiation and do not be tempted to go outside of them. You do not want to work for next door to nothing, nor do you want to price yourself out of the market. You need to understand your own value and be sure of yourself when you agree a price for your own services.

When signing the contract, ideally ensure that all owners are party to it and have signed. Agree how they would like to have viewings conducted, whether or not they would consider having an Open Day. Very importantly, if you are going to be conducting viewings for the client, you will need to ensure that you follow the procedures for key collection, recording, safe-keeping and return are followed precisely. It is your responsibility to ensure that you know what these procedures are.

Vendors and landlords often ask two or three agents to visit their property so you may come away without having closed the deal. You must make a note in your diary to ring them back to see whether they are still considering or if they have given the deal to another agent. If they have, then politely ask for feedback i.e. why did they make that decision? It could be that they have a relative who has a favourite agent and they decide to use them but if it is something you can improve upon then you will be better armed next time!

Remember that clients' information is confidential so great care should be taken to ensure that records are kept securely and that they cannot fall into other people's hands. You must also make sure that you do not divulge information in conversation to friends or family as you may contravene the Data Protection Act – refer to Section on Legislation. Records must be kept as per the recommended procedures and as with keys, it is your responsibility to ensure that this is done correctly.

BE EQUIPPED TO PRESENT YOUR PROPERTY PORTFOLIO TO BEST ADVANTAGE AND KNOW HOW TO SELL!

MARKETING YOUR PROPERTIES

You have just taken on a property, the contract is signed and you are ready to go. So how do you make sure you present your property to its best advantage?

The Brochure

The most important aspect of your advertising is your brochure, on-line and hard copy and it needs meticulous planning.

Before taking photographs, if possible you can 'dress' the house by asking your client to make sure there is as little clutter as possible, cushions arranged, personal items placed attractively and curtains hung straight. Other simple things you can do are:

- **'Staging'** Remember first impressions count – keep front garden clear of clutter, weeded, with pots having dead flowers removed.
- Lawns should be mown, borders weeded, hedges cut and clutter cleared.
- Clean windows and make sure curtains and vases etc., look appealing from the outside.
- De-clutter rooms and consider removing very personal objects including photographs,

remembering that nothing should be moved without the clients' consent and approval.

- Bathrooms, kitchens, bedrooms should contain items as appropriate – bathrooms should have toilet lids down, shower curtains straight, bath mats uncrumpled, bedrooms should have made beds, curtains drawn back, no clothes left around, kitchens should not have stacked plates and cups waiting to be washed up, and should look clean and tidy.
- **Photographs** need to be appealing and listen to you client carefully and ask for their opinion on what features they believe are the most important to emphasise. Ask them what aspects of the property had been the deciding factors on whether or not to buy or rent. This is likely to appeal to other buyers or renters too.
- Sunny days are best for taking external pictures, and ask owners to remove cars from drives, mowers from lawns (after having been used!), general garden tidy so that the aspect is clear and clutter free.
- Flowers enhance the attractiveness of rooms.
- Conservatories need to show their best features and photographs work best if taken from outside looking in
- Remember that mirrors and windows can produce undesired effects. It is not uncommon for an agent to return to download pictures to find an image of a client or themselves in the reflection!

- Internal - stage a room (with the vendor's agreement), remove items of furniture, clear surfaces (especially in kitchens and bathrooms) take up rugs, remove kid's toys/dog's basket. Move some greenery into the room and turn on all lights.
- Make sure you are fully conversant with how the camera operates so that you can be professional in your approach and make sure it has plenty of battery so that you are not left with a red face. Make sure the lens is clean.
- A room can appear larger if you stand in the corner of a room showing two walls and a piece of the ceiling.
- You can show the vendor or landlord the pictures before leaving and discuss which ones should be used

Measurements MUST be accurate – so take your time and record each room and area carefully. Do the descriptions at the same time and remember that you must not describe laminated wood as wood or central heating throughout if it is only partial for example.

Accuracy in recording property details is of the utmost importance as you must not mislead or misrepresent any aspects. Before putting the house up for sale or letting you must include an up to date Energy Performance Certificate (EPC).

When your brochure has been proof read, print off a

perfectly presented copy then ask the vendor or landlord to check it and sign it off as being correct.

The Marketing Plan

You will already have discussed and noted your marketing plan with the client. You now need to ensure that the property gets as much exposure to potential buyers or renters as soon as possible. Before you advertise at all though, you must ensure you have all the facts correct and agreed, completed your records as per procedures and have a signed sales or letting agreement with the vendor.

Viewings

The aim of the viewing is of course to make a sale or let, so you should be well prepared to answer any questions that a potential buyer or tenant will ask. Your skills at rapport building will be all important so that you can determine how serious the viewer is in wanting to purchase or rent, their reasons for it and their intended timescale. In the case of a potential purchaser you can ask whether or not they have sold their property – it could be an opportunity for you or a colleague.

Even if your viewer does not want to go ahead with the sale or rent then the time can be used profitably to determine more clearly what the client is looking for so that you can look for something that will more closely match their requirements.

Remember that the way you conduct viewings is likely to

leave a lasting impression and this could lead to recommendations to others and referrals.

Points to Remember

- Make sure you are fully conversant with all the notes on the property that you have on file and also the area. To do a professional viewing you need to confidently answer all questions that are likely to be asked, including the type of central heating and its age, double glazing, transport links and local schools, likely costs of gas or electricity bills, and if renting or buying a flat what arrangements there are for maintenance and costs.
- Before doing the viewing make sure you have contact details and telephone them before you leave to check the time they will expect you. You will need to have advised the property owner of the time of viewings giving them notice that has been agreed if necessary. This should always be during daylight hours unless impossible.
- Dress smartly with clean shoes and take some covers with you so that both you and your viewers do not walk dirty shoes on to clean floors.
- Make sure you know any security codes to gain entry and that you have taken the correct key with you. Take a smart folder with a brochure for the viewer and any other relevant details.
- Introduce yourself and give out your business card. If the landlord, tenant or vendor of the property is

there, introduce them and make sure you remember the arrangements that had been agreed for viewing.
- If the property is empty – make sure you put lights on in rooms, open curtains and ensure that everything looks as good as possible without disturbing the owner's possessions. Make sure that you remember to put things back as they were when you leave, lights off, security codes back on etc.
- It's always a good idea to show the room that has a 'wow' factor first – or at least the room that is most likely to appeal. Take your time to allow the viewer to appreciate all aspects of the property as you go around. Return to the best room of the house when you have finished the viewing.
- Point out all the positive features including economic benefits, whether or not the garden is south facing, good insulation etc. Anything negative that is pointed out, try to turn it around in to a positive if possible, or without contradicting the viewer, at least try to explain why it might not be a problem.
- Make sure of your facts – if you are unsure of anything despite your research and reading of the file – go back to the office, check it out and get back to the viewer later.
- Review what is positive about the property mentioning any good things that were noted by the viewer.

- Ask the client if they think they might like to make an offer to buy or want to take the property.
- Depending on whether they want to buy or rent, let them know what will happen next and arrange another appointment if appropriate.
- Contact the landlord or owner after the viewing to give them feedback. Feedback is crucial not only to demonstrate your professionalism, but also act upon anything that could improve a future viewing.

Make sure that notes are made on file and on line for the property/vendor/landlord records immediately after the viewing.

HAVE AN UNDERSTANDING OF THE ART AND IMPORTANCE OF NEGOTIATION ON BEHALF OF YOUR CLIENT AND HOW TO CLOSE DEALS

The Offer and Acceptance

Getting an offer is the start of a process that needs to be managed sensitively and competently throughout.

As you gain experience you will begin to gauge the best moment to ask the viewer if they would like to make an offer. You should do this while you are in the most attractive part of the property and a good way of approaching the question is to ask what they most like about it. If they mention things they don't like, you could perhaps suggest ways these could be rectified relatively simply or inexpensively if this is possible. They could take this cost in to account when making an offer so this is something you could tell them.

If an offer is made, and it is often a 'first' offer, you must make a record as per procedures and put it to your vendor immediately. Negotiating means understanding what a good offer is and advising your vendor accordingly. If you judge it to be a good offer then you should say so and try to persuade the vendor to accept. If however you feel that the vendor should and could get an offer nearer to the actual asking price then your job is to explain why and suggest that you go back to the buyer with a figure higher than the original offer.

This is where the real negotiating skill comes in – where you balance what the buyer is able and willing to pay – with the needs of the vendor to make a sale at a good price. You do not want to be in a position where you lose a sale by advising the vendor to stick to the original price for example – but usually a little give and take on both sides is possible. You will need to use your judgement wisely. If a low offer is made you can ask the buyer directly if they would go higher if the vendor refuses. This will help you deal confidently with your vendor when putting the offer forward.

Ultimately, however, the decision is the vendors and if they want to accept a price that you think is ridiculously low, and you have advised them not to by giving the reasons why, then you will have fulfilled your obligations. But remember that your job is to get the best deal for the vendor that you can.

And finally, when you get to the negotiation stage make sure that whatever time of day it is you should try to go back straight away to vendor and buyer until a deal is struck. Keeping your clients waiting for answers gives them time to reconsider, dither, change their minds especially if they start discussing it with family and friends. You need to get the deal agreed as fast as you can providing you are sure that both parties are satisfied – strike while the iron is hot and you will be well on the way to successful completion!

STEER YOUR SALES THROUGH TO SUCCESSFUL COMPLETION BY UNDERSTANDING THE IMPORTANCE OF EFFECTIVE COMMUNICATION

Sale Accepted

Once the offer has been made and accepted, your main role has ended and that of the two parties' solicitors begins. Remember that the property should not be taken off the market until the offer and acceptance letters have been sent out and the notification of sale letters sent to vendor, buyer, and their solicitors.

After the necessary acceptance letters and notification of sale have been issued the rest of the proceedings are under control of the solicitors involved.

However, this is not the end of the estate agent's work and the next part is what counts towards the actual completion of the sale.

It is up to you to keep up to speed with progress of the sale and to liaise between vendor, buyer and sometimes their solicitors to ensure that everything is moving smoothly. If it isn't and there are things that you can do to move things forward then you should do so. Details of progress should be recorded so that you are aware when contracts will be exchanged and completed. As the agent handling the property, you will be aware of the full sale history and know the personalities involved. You must always remember though that you have an agreement with the Vendor and it is therefore the Vendor's interests you must have uppermost in your mind from start to finish to ensure you get the best deal for them.

You may often have contact with Mortgage Lenders, Surveyors or Banks as well as with solicitors. If these professionals are those you have recommended then it will make life easier as you will have built up a relationship with them. Hopefully, through previous completed contracts you will know that you can rely on the speed and efficiency of their service. When using these tried and tested professionals, you can confidently them to clients with confidence and earn some extra money at the same time.

Cash Buyers

Someone comes along and assures you they are going to

pay cash for a sale property so the transaction should go through smoothly and quickly. Sounds great but a word of caution is needed though as it is essential that in such cases, as well as with mortgages, that you have evidence that the buyer actually does have ready access to cash. You will need to ask for a letter or statement from a bank, solicitor or mortgage lender to show that the money is, or will be, available as soon as the contract is ready to complete. Such evidence should be made available to you before you put the house under offer – until you have proof of ability to purchase you should carry on marketing.

Remember always that you are acting for the Vendor in the negotiation as they are your client NOT the buyer.

There are other methods of selling a house other than a straightforward For Sale price and these are briefly outlined below.

Sales by Auction

At some stage you may be asked about whether or not they should sell their house by auction. Auction sales need a completely different set of professional skills and this is not something you will get involved in. You should suggest selling through your company but if it does not sell then they could consider auction as a last resort. It is likely that a vendor would get less at auction than through the other routes outlined above and below.

Sales by 'Sealed Bid'

You might be asked by a vendor to put their property up for tender under a sealed bid process. In this case the property will be advertised as such and potential purchasers invited to make bids for the property by a set date. The process for bidding will be set out precisely with the closing date and time. The vendor is not obliged to take the highest bid as it may be that other factors e.g. completion date that could be met would make a lower bid more attractive.

It is not good practice to consider bids that are submitted after the closing date although the agent still has a legal duty to put any offer before the vendor. This could however, lead to an unsavoury situation where one potential buyer is vying with another. You should obtain in writing from the vendor a statement saying that no more bids will be accepted after the agreed date and then you will have done all you can to avoid the problem. As soon as an offer has been accepted, all parties who have bid should be notified of their success or otherwise. Solicitors will then be instructed as for a normal sale.

Sales at 'Fixed Price'

Vendors will sometimes state a price that they will accept but not go underneath this. The first person to offer the price is usually accepted providing that the sale and completion go ahead within an agreed time-scale. Potential buyers are still likely to make offers below the fixed price and as an agent you are still obliged to notify the vendor.

Sales without Viewing – 'Expressions' or 'Notes of Interest'

Sometimes, a sale can take place without the buyer viewing it and they may just note interest in a property because either it is well known to them, or they are fully confident that they will be getting a good deal e.g. an experienced property developer who would want to be advised of any details regarding the property.

Often the potential purchaser's solicitor will make the note of interest formally, and this means that you will normally be obliged to keep the solicitor informed of any details or developments regarding the sale of the property.

Sales Priced as 'Offers Over'

A property can be put up for sale with an 'offers over' price. This is to try to get potential buyers to offer higher and thus not invite offers under the price – although in practice this still does happen and of course you are duty bound to put these offers before the vendor.

A Few Common Factors Influencing the Speed and Outcome of a Sale

Chains

Quite often there will be a 'chain' of buyers and vendors, and the more there are the more likelihood of complications and sometimes breakdown if one or more parties decides they cannot or will not proceed for some reason. One of the main reasons you must keep in contact with your buyer and vendor and the respective solicitors is to watch out for signs of anything going wrong. You may need to keep in mind another interested buyer of a property if there is one, who could potentially be approached if an expected sale goes through.

Mortgages

Sometimes there may be a delay whilst someone's mortgage comes through. As long as the mortgage lender provides you with a letter showing that a mortgage has been 'agreed in principle' then you can stop marketing the property and expect the sale to go ahead.

Surveys

Mortgages are almost always 'subject to survey' meaning that if anything dire is found e.g. subsidence, or excessive amounts of asbestos that would most likely need removal by specialists then a sale could break down.

UNDERSTAND THE IMPORTANCE OF KEEPING ACCURATE RECORDS AND KNOW HOW AND WHEN TO DO IT

Records of the property, the vendor, all viewings and the eventual offer through to completion of sale must be meticulously kept. If you are not around, anyone should be able to refer to the file to enable them to pick up precisely where you left off seamlessly.

Not only are the records for convenience for you and your colleagues, but they are vital evidence should there be any complaint or questions about the way the sale proceeded.

In addition, records showing the names and contact details of viewers will provide you with potential buyers should a sale fall through for any reason.

Make sure that you are fully conversant with the methods of record keeping and if in doubt always ask your manager. Do not attempt to guess that you are doing it right if you are not 100% sure.

The whole of the sales process from start to finish should be conducted courteously, efficiently and professionally. Consistency of attitude will result in your clients keeping a good memory of their dealings with you and they are much more likely to use you again or refer your services to others.

MASTER THE RUDIMENTS OF PROPERTY LEGISLATION

Remember that it is your responsibility to understand property legislation and there are essential websites for you to refer to and understand.

We recommend you visit The Property Ombudsman website for guidance on the current legislation http://www.tpos.co.uk

Further information is also available at professionalpropertyacademy.co.uk or on one of our advanced courses.

Summary of Sales Procedure

1. Conduct Valuation
2. Sign up Vendor
3. Obtain ID and proof of residence
4. Create details and photograph
5. Check/Order EPC
6. Obtain vendor brochure approval
7. Publish property
8. Book viewings
9. Carry out viewings
10. Follow Up Viewings
11. Handle Offers
12. Progress sale Notification of Sale etc.

Conclusion and Further Study

We hope you have found this guide useful as a starting point for your new career. We cannot possible cover every subject in this book and recommend you attend one of our courses.

The **Quick Start Letting System** (Q.S.L.) is a comprehensive lettings training program that gives you the tools and information to start trading today.

For those looking for the next level **The Ultimate Property Profit Masterclass** is a four day training program covering all aspects of sales and lettings and how to grow your team and your business.

**For all the details visit
ProfessionalAgentAcademy.co.uk**

Made in the USA
Charleston, SC
22 November 2015